T0208224

ATTRACT SUCCESS EVERY DAY

8 STEPS FOR BUILDING THE LIFE OF YOUR DREAMS

MENACOLE O'SULLIVAN

authorHOUSE®

AuthorHouse™
1663 Liberty Drive
Bloomington, IN 47403
www.authorhouse.com
Phone: 1-800-839-8640

First published by AuthorHouse 2/15/2011

ISBN: 978-1-4567-3827-3 (sc)
ISBN: 978-1-4567-3828-0 (e)

Library of Congress Control Number: 2011901715

Printed in the United States of America

To my beloved grandmother Lillian Reid, who taught me so much about life and going for what you want. You were such an inspiration and a good role model. You will forever be in my heart and in my thoughts. I miss you so much.

TABLE OF CONTENTS

ACKNOWLEDGEMENTS

First and foremost I thank and acknowledge my beautiful mother Pearlma, whose tenacity and sacrifice made it possible for me to be where I am today. Though we sometimes have our differences, I will forever be grateful for everything you do for me.

I would also like to thank my second mom, Velma Morgan whose kind and nurturing ways inspire me to be strong. Thanks for being there for me and for being who you are. You are such as source of motivation to me.

I would also like to thank my father, Norman O'Sullivan. I admire your creativity and resourcefulness. Thank you for being there when I need someone to talk to or a second opinion.

Thank you Mar and Racquel for your kindness and encouragement. I am blessed to have sisters like you.

My cousin Pearl Dawkins, thanks for your positive energy and encouragement. Your kindness and patience is such a good role model. Thanks for being you.

A big thank you to my dear friends and editors: Debbie

Sinclair, Nicole Sidhu, Glenn Ryan, Marielee O'Sullivan and Jane Catalan. Thank you for your time and great feedback in helping me to make this book the best it could be. Your words of wisdom and encouragement were the wind beneath my wings.

Thank you Pat Mirjah for being a source of inspiration. I will be forever grateful for your words of wisdom.

To the team at Author House, thank you very much. A special thanks to Jenn Handy for your follow through and professionalism, it's been such a pleasure working with you.

I would also like to thank my first readers, my friends. Your enthusiasm to read the book pushed me to get it out. You guys are great at keeping me accountable. Thanks for being my extended marketing team!

INTRODUCTION

A lot of people are busy chasing success and are frustrated because things aren't working out the way they want. Success eludes them like a butterfly. With all the hype about the "law of attraction" and thinking your way into whatever you want, people still aren't getting the results they seek.

You've probably heard the phrase, "thoughts become things." But is that all there is to getting what you want? You mean to tell me that all I have to do is think about becoming a millionaire and I'll just get the money! Well then, how come I don't have it yet? I've been thinking about it for a while now. As Cuba Gooding Jr. would say, "Show me the money!"

You've probably experienced the same thing yourself and still haven't "attracted" what you want. Perhaps you just haven't figured out "the secret." Unlike popular beliefs, thoughts alone don't become things. Action is required. It's very unlikely that you will have a windfall brought to your feet by just sitting on your butt and daydreaming. But does this mean that you have to chase success? If it won't land on your lap you probably need to pursue it, right? Success is not something you pursue. Much like chasing a butterfly, it can prove to be futile.

So what's the point of this book? To bash success? Or bash the "law of attraction?" Not quite. But it doesn't promote wishful thinking either. After reading this book you will have the fundamentals to build the lifestyle you want. This is not some hype or gimmick to tickle your ears. What you'll learn is based on solid principles that have stood the test of time. Practical nuggets that when applied, will bring the results you want. As you read on, you'll come to appreciate the beauty of compound interest when you have it working in your favor. I'm not just talking in financial terms. After all, there is more to success than money.

In life we get what we deserve. This means that the seeds we sow today will determine the crop we'll reap tomorrow. As the saying goes, "you can't plant corn if it's peas you want to reap!" We get what we deserve! Not out of mere self-centeredness or egotism but based on the seeds we plant by our activity. Wishful thinking and daydreaming is not the way to go if you want tangible results to last a lifetime. *Someday, I'll go to Japan. Someday I'll start my own business… someday…* No, no, no my friend! The *someday* wishful thinking approach just won't cut it!

If you want to become a basketball player you must master the fundamentals of the game. You have to know how to shoot hoops. But knowing alone isn't enough. Mastery is important. You have to practice shooting from different angles to dunk the ball in the hoop when the competition gets tight and you have less than two seconds to win or lose the game. Life itself is like a game. That's why it's important to know the fundamental rules so you can use them to your advantage.

A few simple things practiced every day can make all the difference in how your life turns out. By reading this book you will come to know those things so you can spend most of your time doing them. Attracting the success you want is not a mystery. It's not hard either. In fact it's quite easy. That's because it's something that you *can do*. However, don't be fooled by the word *easy*. Sometimes what's easy *to do* is also easy *not to do* and this is where people mess up. But that doesn't have to be you.

You picked up this book because you are determined to build a better life for yourself. By applying what you learn from this book, you'll be able to do that. Unlike winning the lottery, success is not by chance. It's achievable, without guesswork. You can have the lifestyle, the relationships and the income you want. Just turn the page to find out how…

Chapter 1

Decide What You Want

A dear friend once told me, "Success is something you attract by the person you become."

When I first heard those words, they really hit me. They made me think long and hard. As I pondered I kept asking myself, "What does that really mean? What kind of person would I need to become to attract the success I want?" Urged by my curiosity, my search for the meaning of those words began. In time I learned that the goals we set for ourselves and what we do each day determines our outcome. Our surroundings, friends, books, magazines, music, movies, and even video games influence the decisions we make and who we ultimately become.

We're affected by what we see, hear and feel. Unless we consciously choose how we want our lives to be, we'll just drift along with little or no sense of direction. If we don't know where we're going, then any road is good enough. More than likely, we'll end up where we don't want to be.

However, when we take the time to decide what we want and work towards its attainment, we take control of our lives and where we end up. We become the creator of our own destiny. Instead of just drifting with the current, we chart our own course.

When we decide what we want and write them down, we set our goals. But what power do goals have? Why are they important? Simply put, we create our future in advance by the goals we set for ourselves. We create our destiny. We mold and shape our lives. Our goals become the map that guides us towards our destination. As we chart our course, our goals help us to stay on track. They help us develop confidence, personal power and drive. They give us something to look forward to.

In 1953, a study about goal setting was conducted with the graduating class of a leading University. Of the graduates that were surveyed, only 3% had written goals with a specific plan to achieve them. The other 97% of graduates didn't have clear, written goals. They just had a general idea of what they wanted. Twenty years later, a follow up study was conducted. The results of the study were amazing. When questioned on happiness, health and so on, the results were subjective. However, a measurable result was the net worth of the graduates. The financial wealth of the 3% that had clearly defined goals and a plan to achieve them was worth more than that of the remaining 97% combined. Think of it...The 3% that had clear, written goals had more money than the combined net worth of the 97% who didn't have written goals! Incredible isn't it? That's the difference goals can make.

Set your goals so it will be easy to track your progress. Make SMART goals. This basically means that your goals are:

Specific –	You have clearly defined what you want.
Measurable –	It's easy to track your progress.
Attainable –	Your goal is within your reach.
Realistic –	What you've identified can be achieved when you want it to.
Time-sensitive –	You have a target date to accomplish what you want.

WRITE DOWN YOUR GOALS

The mere act of writing something down creates a deeper impression in your mind. People who write down their dreams and aspirations are more likely to fulfill them than those who don't. That's regardless of the goal or dream. That's why it's important to write down your goals. So grab a pen and a notebook. As we examine the five core areas of life, write down your goals for each category:

1. Spiritual
2. Financial
3. Relationships
4. Career
5. Health

1. WHAT ARE YOUR SPIRITUAL GOALS?

Let's face it. Not everyone views spirituality as being important. However, building a relationship with our Creator yields many rich rewards. That's why it's good to cultivate such a relationship. There's a certain inner calm and peace that comes from filling our spiritual need.

What kind of relationship would you like to have with your Creator? It's good to take the time to think about this. From personal experience, the quality of my life has improved significantly since I have started reading the Bible daily and reflecting on what I read. You too can experience the blessings and inner peace that comes from drawing close to God. For example, you could set a goal to read one chapter of the Bible each day.

2. WHAT DO YOU WANT FINANCIALLY?

We all need money to survive. It is an essential part of life. Some people have mixed feelings about money. Others find it noble to be poor. They think it's materialistic and selfish to be rich. As a result, a lot of people don't even want to talk about money. It's like a sacred subject that should never be discussed. On the other extreme, some people spend their lives chasing after money. Making money becomes their chief aim in life. In their greed for money and what it can buy, they alienate people around them and take their loved ones for granted.

Neither of the two extremes is healthy. Constantly worrying about money, because you have too little or because you have too much, is not productive. Like any other tool, money must be handled with care. This is especially important to avoid undue stress. Just as how a butcher needs to handle the chopper carefully so he doesn't cut off his fingers, money must be handled with care so we don't sever important relationships or cause harm to ourselves.

There's nothing wrong with having lots of money. However, it's good to have a balanced view of money. Unlike popular beliefs, money in of itself is not the root of evil. The **love of money** is what we need to be careful of. The Bible says *"Those who are determined to be rich fall into temptation and a snare and many senseless and hurtful desires, which plunge men into destruction and ruin. For the love of money is a root of all sorts of injurious things, and by reaching out for this love some have …stabbed themselves all over with many pains."* (2 Timothy 6:10-11)

Being rich doesn't necessarily mean being greedy. It's okay to have financial abundance. After all, some people inherit wealth. Others earn it by rendering honest service to others. However, the key is to put the right priority and value on money. Earning an income should not be at the sacrifice of other important things in our life. It shouldn't be at the loss of someone else's life savings. Neither should its acquisition cause harm to others.

We need to exercise good judgment when it comes to acquiring money so that we don't miss out on other important aspects of our lives like our spirituality or a good relationship with others. As we strive to make a living we need to bear in mind that money is just a tool to enable us to care for ourselves and our families. Of course it's also important to give back and help others as our circumstances permit.

To be good at any trade, you need to acquire new skills. The same principle applies to money. You need to acquire some financial smarts to get good at using money wisely.

Make it a practice to keep a part of all you earn. Start where you can but strive to set aside ten percent or more. Basically for every dollar you make, put aside ten cents. This will mean that you have to develop self-control to avoid spending everything. The good thing about this is that you will have some money left over which will make you feel better over time as it starts to add up.

However, if you fail to do this you could become enslaved to debt. Then much of your focus will be on your bills which in turn will sap your energy and squeeze the joy out of life. It will be like you're on a treadmill that never stops. Instead of being excited to wake up each day, you'll dread getting up. However, if that's how you feel right now, don't be discouraged. If you wise up, you can reverse that and turn things around. You will just need to pay close attention to what you are reading now and actually apply it.

Okay. It's time to write down your financial goals. Write down where you are now and where you want to be. Then write down a few actions you will take to get you to where you want to be. Just remember, only money gained from honest efforts will last so make sure the steps you have in mind are legal and ethical!

3. HOW GOOD DO YOU WANT YOUR RELATIONSHIPS TO BE?

No one is an island. We all need a sense of connection with others to feel complete. Even the shyest person needs to be loved and touched. We are born with the need to connect with others. However, we also need time alone to refresh our spirit. As you write your relationship goals, be sure to set goals to build up: 1) yourself, 2) your family and 3) your friends.

4. WHAT DO YOU WANT TO DO AS A CAREER?

Remember when you were a kid? Can you recall what you wanted to be when you grew up? Back then everything seemed possible. You didn't even wonder how it was going to happen. You just knew things would work out. When you were done talking, everyone believed you. You spoke with passion, a sense of purpose and a sense of pride. What about now? Are you doing what you want to do? Or did you give up on your dreams? Did life get in the way?

If you're not doing what you would like to do, it's still within reach. *You can still realize your dreams.* It's not too late. If 70 and 80 year olds can go back to school and complete their High School Diploma or graduate from University, you can do whatever you're still dreaming of doing!

Take the founder of Kentucky Fried Chicken (KFC) for example. Colonel Saunders never gave up on his dreams. Even in his sixties he still cherished his dreams and took steps to make them come true. Today, KFC is a worldwide phenomenon because he never viewed himself as too old to go for what he wanted.

Another example is Thomas Edison, the inventor of the light bulb. Before he figured out how to make bulbs, he first discovered over a thousand ways *not* to create the light bulb. Yet those 'failed' experiments didn't deter him. He kept going. He didn't waste his time talking to himself about why he couldn't do it. He just kept going until he did. Just take a page from his book and learn from him. Never give up on yourself!

But what if you're already doing what you want to do? Is there anything else you would like to accomplish? Anything you want to change? Think about it. If there's anything you still want to go for, just put it in writing and go for it. Go ahead… get your pen and paper. Write down what you want. Next write down how you plan to go about getting there.

Just remember to never use your age as an excuse to avoid going after your dreams. Regardless or whether you think you're too young or you're too old. Just set your goals and do one thing each day towards it. Before you know it, you will have some good momentum going and each day you will get closer and closer towards fulfilling your dream!

5. WHAT KIND OF HEALTH DO YOU WANT?

I don't know about you, but I like having nice flat abs and a toned body. I'm also a straight woman so I pay attention to how men carry themselves. In men, I like a nice six pack and muscular biceps. You can laugh. I was laughing too when I wrote this. Physically, I'm drawn to that stuff. Of course, a handsome face is also a given.

Very few people have the natural metabolism that requires little effort to maintain a nice physique. Besides, our bodies change as we grow. So it does take some effort to maintain the kind of look that you want. One of the things that I constantly strive for is the same physique and energy level that I had as a teenager. I'm taller now, so I have grown out of most of my clothes. But it still feels good to be able to try on a dress that I wore when I was nineteen and know it still fits. On the other hand, I don't mind giving up some lousy habits that I've had since I was young. One particular weakness I can think of is my love for sweets. I love candies. This doesn't go so well when you have a family history of diabetes. To help me stay in shape I set health goals, monitor what I eat and exercise regularly.

What about you? Have you thought about your health goals? What kind of body do you want? How low do you want to keep your cholesterol level? How about your blood pressure? Remember there will be sacrifices involved but stay focused on the rewards at the end.

It's also important to build friendships with people who enjoy working out and eating healthy. If you can find one or more reliable friends with similar health goals as you, partner up with them. It's good to have someone to hold you accountable. Having one or more friends to hold you accountable could mean the difference between sticking to your goals versus giving up.

Being healthy goes beyond what you look like. That's why it's important to feed your mind and nourish your emotions. What you feed your mind with affects your outlook on life. In turn, your outlook affects your physical health. How many books would you like to read per month? How often do you want to go out and socialize? These are both factors that affect your health.

Take the time now to jot down some health goals. Set some goals to improve your physical, emotional and mental well being. Then act in harmony with your goals. It's pointless to have a goal to lose weight then feast on burgers all day long and never exercise. So make sure your actions support your goals.

As you work on your written goals, your efforts will compound. Over time you will attract what you want by the actions you take. This will prove true in all areas that you focus on. Yes, it takes focus and discipline. That's the part of the puzzle that makes it all work!

Notes

CHAPTER 2

BELIEVE IN YOURSELF

"It's not who you are that holds you back, it's who you think you're not." ~Author Unknown

The main reason people hold back from going after their dreams can be summed up in one word: *fear*. Fear of failure. Fear of the unknown. Fear of what their family and friends will think. Before embarking on their dreams they hesitate, often thinking *what if I lose all my money? What if I don't make it? What if I get sick? What if? What if? What if…*

It's natural to feel nervous when undertaking an endeavor that takes you out of your comfort zone. This is where the element of fear comes in. It's not that you can't do something. In most instances the actual work is quite easy to do. Yet, if you give way to doubt, it's easier to not even try.

SOMETIMES IT TAKES COURAGE

Personally, I'm a pretty outgoing person who makes friends easily. Recently, I went to an event for some spiritual encouragement and to make some new friends. The first half of the event was good. I took notes diligently as I listened to each speaker. I was totally in my element as I took notes. Though I went to the event by myself, there were about nine hundred other people present. A pretty good size crowd. Hence, there was plenty of opportunity to fulfill my second objective to make new friends.

The real test came at lunch time when it was time to get up and branch out to make friends. Now, I'm not a shy person but in that moment I was both shy and nervous. A million thoughts ran through my mind. *Who do I talk to first? What will I say? There are some young people like me; maybe I'll go talk to them. Oh no, there's too many of them. I'll go later. I don't want to draw too much attention to myself by going over there now.* Those are just a few thoughts that popped in my head. Why was I so nervous? I think it was because I went to the event alone. Because of that, I felt a bit awkward when it was time to strike up a conversation. The funny thing is, when I'm around my friends it's easy to make conversations with strangers. But in this case, the comfort of having someone else there was missing. I felt alone in that moment. As a result, it took a lot more courage to get that first conversation going.

To shake off the nervousness, I got up and went to the bathroom. As I was on my way out of the bathroom, I bumped into an old friend. This is someone I knew from when I was a teenager. We both went to the same high school. The last time I saw her was about five years ago. As I pushed the door open, our eyes connected. In unison we exclaimed, "Oh Hi!"

We were both happy and surprised to see each other. Here was my friend with a newborn baby in one hand and a phone to her ear in the other hand. Using discretion, I just smiled and walked back to my seat. I figured I would try to touch base with her again before the lunch break was up. Her hands were full, and it wasn't a good time to talk. Besides, she was on the phone and it's always best to avoid blocking the bathroom entrance. Blocking it would be an invitation to get run over by someone who really had to use to the bathroom.

I walked away feeling good though. Seeing a familiar face was very encouraging. Though I was by myself, at least I knew one person in the crowd. Shortly after eating lunch, I bumped into my friend again and we were able to catch up. By the time we were done talking, the afternoon session was about to begin. I figured I would make it a point to talk to some new people after the program was over.

Though I was still a bit nervous at the end of the event, I managed to break out of my shy mode. Instead of thinking too much, I decided to just go for it. I'm sure my experience during the lunch break helped. But it still took courage to strike out and talk to new people. After all, I was surrounded by people who had come to the event with their friends and relatives. They were all in their own world with little incentive to branch out. I on the other hand, went to the event with the goal of making new friends. That required some courage. I didn't want to go home with the regret of not even trying.

Once I made up my mind, I stood up, smiled, and then started introducing myself to my neighbors. By taking the first step, my confidence came back. The social butterfly in me came out. Within about ten minutes I made contact with about eight different people. A little later, I was able to have a nice conversation with someone else that I really clicked with. Mission accomplished. I went home feeling great and I had made two good contacts and exchanged phone numbers. Looking back, once I got up and started talking to people, they were so nice and friendly. In no time I was in my element making friends. Once I got started, it got easier and easier. Getting started was the hard part.

FEEL THE FEAR AND DO IT ANYWAY

In our fast paced society, it's easy to feel overwhelmed. If we're not careful we could get so bogged down with trivial things that consume our time. Important goals that we may want to do could be crowded out leaving us little time to go after our dreams. Though we would want to go for a deep seated dream or desire, we may become discouraged by the things we already have on our plate. If we think too much about what we're already pursuing, we may delay taking action on our goals, until the "right time." Let's face it. No one wants to start something they believe they will fail at. However, sometimes we just have to decide to win and do what it takes to make it happen.

Recently I found out about a training program at work. It came with a world renowned certification, if you passed the exam on the third and final day of the training. In the marketplace the course is worth several thousand dollars and the certification is very valuable. If taken at work, it would be at no cost to the employee. The course was only three days but it was jam packed with information. As a result, not everyone who took the course passed the exam.

When I first learned about the course, I was right in the middle of writing this book with a target deadline to get it to the publisher. Additionally, I was about a week away from planning a party for over fifty people. I was the chief organizer. The party was my idea and I needed to rehearse a few acts that would be performed at the event.

However, when my co-worker told me about the course, my interest was piqued. Hence, I went online to the training site and started looking up information on how to register for it. At first I couldn't find the course on the training site, so I emailed the training department to express my desire to take it. I told them I couldn't find it online and asked how I could enroll. Very promptly they responded to my inquiry and informed me that the class was full. It wouldn't be until about two to three months later that they would be offering the course again. So they offered to put me on the waiting list, which I gladly accepted.

About four hours later, the training department emailed me back and told me they just had a cancellation and asked if I would like to take the spot. If I did, I would have to start the training in two days and take a one hour exam on the third and final day of the course. I knew of the exam because my workmate who told me about the course was freaking about taking it. Now that I had the option to get into this class, I had to make a decision fast. I wanted to take the training but

I was ok with the two month wait time. After all, I had a lot on my plate and the extra time to prepare would do me well. The excuses just kept flying through my head: *"I have some key meetings this week. In fact I'm the organizer for the meetings and I just booked them. I need to have those meetings. I'll just email and tell them I'll wait for the next course…"*

I had started to type the email when another thought came to me. *"Ask what is the starting and ending time for the training each day."* I listened to my inner voice and asked about the start and end times. A few minutes later they, came back to me and said from 8:30am to 5:00pm each day. I then looked at my calendar and thought about it. There were a few meetings that I could re-arrange to make it work. Before I gave a response, I went over to my manager and briefed him on the exam and the days and times.

Shortly after obtaining approval from my manager, I re-arranged my meetings and confirmed with the training coordinator that I would be able to attend. I only had one day to make up my mind. Once the decision was made, I made myself available. I didn't ask what about those who were ahead of me on the waiting list. Frankly, that was none of my business and I didn't care to know. All I know is that the opportunity presented itself. Instead of putting it off, I decided to seize the opportunity and find a way to make it work. My email went something like this: *"I would love to attend the training. Thanks for considering me. If you could email me back to confirm my registration that would be great."* Within two minutes I got the invitation for each day of the course and an email confirming I was registered. Right away, I accepted the invitation and blocked the time on my calendar.

Getting into the training was one thing. Soaking up all that information in three days was something else! After the first three hours of being in the program, some wild and crazy thoughts started flying through my head: *How are you going to do this? Are you nuts? Don't you have to rehearse every evening this week? The party is on Saturday! When are you going to find time to study for an exam a day before? Your co-worker failed his exam. It's not a walk in the park. You're going to have to focus on this to pass. What are you doing?* However, I ignored my limiting thoughts because I had already made a decision and I was determined to see it through. Before I got accepted in the course my initial thought was, *"If I fail, I can always take the exam again, the next time they offer the course. Two months from now."* However, once I got in, I quickly dismissed that option. Deep down inside, I reasoned to myself: *"I'm not the type to go after something without expecting to win. I've made my decision and I'm shooting to pass. I'm going for bull's eye."*

The first day of the course, I took notes diligently. However, in between I was busy typing the first part of this chapter. I had to complete the book in two weeks and wasn't half way there yet! There I was in the class, multi-tasking away as I listened to the instructor. Since the exam was coming up on the third day, I started 'googling' for online simulation exams. That way, I could get an early start on practicing the exam with mock tests. The instructor made sure to tell us to review the material every night. According to him, the people who failed the exam were mostly those who didn't review the information after the class.

On the second day of the course, I decided to fully immerse myself. I wrote only about one paragraph of my book as most of my attention was focused on preparing for the exam. I wanted to pass, but I was nervous. The sheer volume of information and not knowing what I might be asked on the test made me more anxious. I was starting to feel brain overload. In that moment I wished I could just open my brain, dump everything in it then close it back. I'd then pull out what I needed later on, when I needed to use it. It's too bad as humans we don't have that option! To increase my chances of passing, I decided to study hard, even till late in the night.

It wasn't long before day three rolled in...exam day. I woke up at the crack of dawn and drove in to work. I headed straight for the gym at work and exercised first thing in the morning. I needed to get my adrenaline going to help me with the exam. In no time I was on the treadmill, walking at a brisk speed as I read *The Slight Edge*. I love that book. I first came across it in 2006 when I lived in Northern California. As I savored some nuggets throughout the book, my confidence to take the exam improved. Reading and exercising was my way of getting ready to face the challenge of the day.

The exam was comprised of forty multiple choice questions. We only had an hour to answer them. I must say, I prefer writing essays versus answering multiple choice questions. Primarily because most multiple choice questions are cleverly worded and the answers can be in the grey area at times, based on the choice of words that are used to phrase the questions. I had taken a few simulation exams and passed them so I had grasped the concept of the lessons. However, there were a lot of acronyms to remember and though the number of questions weren't that many, I wanted to remember as much as I could. For multiple choice tests, it's better to know too much and have the option to sort through it, than to know too little.

The last few minutes leading up to the exam were nerve racking. You could almost hear a pin drop in the training room where my colleagues and I were preparing for the big test. You could just feel the tension and anxiety in the room. The same tension you feel when you just want to get something over and done with as fast as possible. The look on everyone's face said it all…They wanted it to be over with just as much as I did.

"You may begin!" The professors said after having us clear our desks of all study materials. His words sounded like gunfire at the beginning of a sprint. Maybe it was due to my nervousness but the way some of the questions were worded, even the answers didn't seem right. However, for those questions I chose what is closest to the truth. Some questions were so easy they seemed like a 'no-brainer'. Overall, I knew the answers to some questions but wasn't quite sure about the answer to others. That made me nervous the whole time. I had to say a quick prayer to calm my nerves. After my silent prayer, I was able to think a little clearer. That enabled me to review the questions with a level head.

Though I finished the exam in less than thirty minutes, I took another twenty minutes to review my answers. Sure enough, as I did that I changed my answers to a few questions. After reviewing my answers over and over, I decided to hit the Submit button and face reality. I eagerly waited in anticipation for the score to return. The response came back in red font. I was already nervous so seeing red font just freaked me out even more! As I looked closer, I saw the words "Congratulations, you have successfully passed the exam." I was ecstatic! My studying and practice tests paid off. I walked out of the room with a sigh of relief. I did it! Tough I had a lot on my plate and could have bailed out at the last minute; I stuck with it and passed the exam. Was it easy? No. But I gave it my best shot and it paid off in the end.

TAKE THE FIRST STEP

It takes courage to believe in yourself and make the most of opportunities when they are presented. It also takes courage to make a decision and follow through on it. In fact, even after you muster up the courage to pursue your dreams, you may feel lonely or nervous at times. Your enthusiasm also could wane after you get started on your dreams. What will you do when that happens? Will you chicken out and quit? Or will you allow fear or the desire to stay in your comfort zone get the better of you? Only you can decide.

However, if you go for your dreams, you will feel a sense of accomplishment and pride after you've gone through the discomfort, experienced the nervousness and then came off victorious. You'll be inspired to take on other challenges from the rewarding results that came after you did all the hard work. After you put in the planning, the sweat and the hours of perfecting your craft. If you quit half way through, you rob yourself of the joy that comes at the end. The reward of feeling happy and fulfilled when your dream finally becomes a reality.

For some goals you'll need a team. That's why building

good relationships with others and nurturing those relationships is very important. However, more than anything else, you'll need faith to believe you can do it. Faith comes from small acts of courage and taking baby steps towards your goals. It's all about the baby steps. The things you do when no one else is there. Things that are easy to do but just as easy not to do. A lot of baby steps, add up to some big steps and major achievements.

Is there something you're thinking of doing but you are hesitant to start? Why not just give it a try? Give it your best effort. You may be pleasantly surprised by the outcome.

NOTES

CHAPTER 3

BUILD YOUR DREAM TEAM

It was mid October when we first started thinking about it. Autumn was at its peak in Oakville, Ontario; the part of Canada where we lived. The rich colors of fall were just magnificent. The trees were a perfect blend of orange, yellow, red, and green. For a good solid six weeks, it was like driving in paradise. The forest looked more like a sea of rich colors that warms the heart as you look at it. To top it all off, the morning sunrise and evening sunset were just spectacular. Talk about paradise. It was like driving in a park every day.

The three of us had decided to meet for a goal-setting workshop at my house. The girls arrived at my house around 6:30 in the evening. It was still nice and light outside. The sun was still out and I had just gotten up from a nap. I went back to bed around 4pm to get a quick nap before they arrived. We had been out in the morning volunteering in our community, teaching others about the Bible. At least those who wanted to learn. We were excited as we planned for the goal-setting workshop. It was something we really looked forward to.

The doorbell rang pronto, on the dot of 6:30pm. I knew because I quickly glanced at the clock on the stove as soon as I heard it. I had just swept the kitchen floor. In the thirty minutes prior to their arrival, I wanted to call them to cancel as I felt like sleeping in some more and just being lazy. Something I hadn't had the luxury of doing for about a month. I was still in my pajamas when they arrived. However, their smiling faces at the door helped me to snap out of my sleepiness. It was time to follow through and have some fun together.

As I opened the door, I greeted the two sisters and led them to their seats around the kitchen table. I then ran upstairs to change and return. I had bought some pretty boxes, magazines, paper glue and fancy writing paper the day before. Each of us girls had also picked up a scrapbook the night before. Today we would start a treasure map and the pretty boxes were to be used as treasure chests to hold pictures and writings that represented our deepest thoughts and desires. We were going to have fun writing our goals for the remainder of the year and the upcoming year. We would also set our three and five year goals. Last but not least, we planned to write down what we wanted in our dream guy since we were still single at the time. Nicole and I were in our twenties and Natasha was still nineteen.

As I prepared the spaghetti squash and shrimps to go with it, the girls wrote down their goals. Nothing was off limits. We each took the time to write out everything we wanted, even if we didn't know how it was going to happen. We looked through the magazines for nice pictures that gave a visual representation of what we wanted. Nice clothes, a house, a car, whatever we thought of. The pictures were then carefully cut out and glued into the scrap book. We only had about an hour together as the two sisters had to meet their mother after.

We wrote down many desires and cut out many pictures. One of the things on our list was to widen out our network of friends and meet some new people. However, we had the most fun, writing about our dream guy on a nice fancy piece of paper. The papers would later go into the safety deposit box I had at the bank. Never to come out again until we had found the guy of our dreams that we were engaged to marry. We shared a few attributes in common in what we wanted and we had fun reading each other's list as we ate dinner. The evening was a success and we looked forward to doing it again soon.

FORMING THE DREAM TEAM

That evening, we planted the seeds of many wonderful things to come in the future. Later that night Nicole and I planned how to start acting on our goal of making new friends. That same evening we came up with a plan. We picked a few dates for different activities. We marked our calendars and started planning for a get together with people we knew and others we wanted to get to know. We planned to include people of all ages: young, old and in-between. Our goal was to get a good number of people together so they could enjoy the evening and we could enjoy their company.

That evening the idea for the party was born. I was able to secure a room for a date that worked well for all three of us. Additionally, I was able to partner up with a few other people to get the invitations out and get the room prepared. A few of our friends volunteered to do live performances which included singing, acting out mini-scripts and poetry. We would also include a little dancing, a quiz and some prizes. We had something to appeal to everyone. Altogether we had about three weeks to pull it off.

With the contribution of the core members of the planning team, the event was a success. The night of the party was beautiful. The turnout was right around what we had anticipated. Everyone was dressed nicely and looked radiant. People mingled comfortably with each other. We all enjoyed a nice buffet of just about every food you could think of. The music was great. The laughter was plenty and the fun was in abundance. There were a few hiccups along the way, but overall it was wonderful. The varied performances kept everyone's attention.

As a team we were able to pull off an event that served the purpose of creating new friends and strengthening the relationships with the ones we knew and were just getting to know. Would it have been as successful if only one of us did everything? Of course not! Did we all benefit and share in the joy of seeing something we imagined come to life? Absolutely! The day after the party we got great feedback. Even people who weren't there commented on how well organized and fun they heard the party was. The event was in good taste and we felt good knowing we made it happen.

Sometimes it takes a team to realize your dream. Why not start building a team of people you can trust? People with similar interests and goals as you. Together you can achieve some great things!

NOTES

CHAPTER 4

TAKE ACTION & STAY FOCUSED

"Doors of opportunity are open to those who continually knock." ~ Jim Rohn

For many people, including me, being consistent can be a challenge. That is one of the reasons why a lot of people miss out on seeing their dreams come to life. It's also one of the reasons why so many people lose money annually on Gym memberships. When we're excited, it's easy to start something. We may even go at it successfully for a week, a month, a year or even several years. And then stop.

Why is that? It could be for just about any reason. But more often than not it's because we lose commitment, and in turn lose our drive. If we don't feel like doing something we simply don't do it. Even though we know we should do it. By not doing what we should do, neglect and mediocrity takes over. Sooner or later, years go by and the pain of regret gets heavier than a ton of bricks.

As the saying goes, a body in motion stays in motion. To be successful at any endeavor you must be disciplined and consistent in the right activities that will give you the desired results. Writing this book for example took a great deal of self disciple. There were some days when I didn't feel like writing. I must admit I've started and stopped writing several books before completing any. However, for this book, I made a commitment to myself and found someone to hold me accountable, and then I finally buckled down and saw it through. I'm proud to say this is my first published book.

Keep Knocking and you'll Find Open Doors

Now and again you hear of someone who, despite humble beginnings and little or no connections, becomes a great success in life. They achieve success by accomplishing what they set out to do. The painter becomes a known artist whose work is valued by many. The little girl with the powerful voice and talent for playing the guitar or piano is discovered. The disabled person is able to overcome his disability and positively contribute to society. All of these are different success stories. But did they come about by chance or luck? Did each of these people just happen to get a "lucky break" that led to fame and fortune? Hardly!

As a child growing up in Jamaica, I recall a little saying on the cover page my notebooks when I was in primary school. It goes something like this: *"The heights of great men reached and kept, were not attained by sudden flight. But they, while their companions slept, were toiling upwards through the night."* I first became aware of that at very young age, about age six. Yet it's still stuck in my brain, many years later.

If you look closely at the thought again, it brings out some very interesting points. The first sentence is packed with insight. *"The heights of great men reached and kept, were not attained by sudden flight."* Not only did these people become great at their chosen field, they were able to maintain their greatness. Was it from a big "lucky break" like winning the lottery? Flat out, no! The little saying goes on to tell us that it took effort and it took time. It says of the great men: *"but they while their companions slept were toiling upwards through the night."*

They were discreet in how they went about their business. However, it wasn't until their efforts started to bear fruit that they became noticed. They toiled for some time. While others were enjoying a comfortable sleep, they were busy sharpening their skills, and perfecting their craft. In time they became great. After the hard work was already invested.

Likewise, to make your dreams come true, you will need to apply daily discipline and focus. It will take time. You will need to work hard at the things that are easy to do but just as easy not to do. Much of your work will go unnoticed for some time, but as long as you remain consistent and optimistic, you will reap the fruits of your labor.

Persistence Pays

I'm sure you've heard the phrase, "Ask and you shall receive. Seek and you shall find. Knock and the door will be open." Yet too often, people don't *persist* is asking. They don't *continue* to seek. Too quickly they stop knocking. We've been conditioned in our society to go for instant gratification. Unlike children who keep asking even after you tell them no a million times, some adults give up at the first sign of struggle. If a child is determined to have something, it doesn't matter how many times you tell her no, it goes in one ear and out the other. Though she may give you a break for a while, she always comes back again. She'll come back asking, seeking and knocking. No to her just means no for now, the yes is coming later. She keeps seeking that yes until she gets it.

We can learn a thing or two from children. To succeed at anything worthwhile, toiling and delayed gratification are all part of the process. It will involve time and it will require a thick skin. A thick skin to keep going in the face of adversity and lack of interest. A thick skin so you keep trying again and again, even after you're discouraged from hearing no several times. As mentioned before, it will also take time. So you will need to view time as an ally. When you first start to knock and you don't hear a response, it's easy to conclude no one is behind the door. However, you may get a response by knocking from different angles, at different times, and at several doors. Eventually a door of opportunity will open. And if you keep going at it, even more doors could open up.

To get a good idea you may have to search for it by listening to others, reading good books or trying new things. You will also need to observe and model other people who've already been successful at what you're trying to do. By sharpening your skills, putting them to use and rendering more service than is required you will become noticed in time.

Your reputation will likely precede you as you look for

doors of opportunity. That's why it's important to maintain your integrity. Who you become in the pursuit of your goals will often determine your outcome so pay attention to who you become. Anything received through lies and deceit usually is usually short-lived. So strive to be a workman with nothing to be ashamed of. Someone who toiled honestly throughout the night, taking baby steps day after day. Someone who persisted through the setbacks but never lost hope. As long as you keep working on your goals, you will be rewarded in time. You just have to stay focused and keep at it.

NOTES

CHAPTER 5

TREAT THE PAST AS A SCHOOL

"When one door of happiness closes, another opens, but often we look so long at the closed door that we do not see the one that has been opened for us."
~Helen Keller

A lot of people beat themselves up about past mistakes and past failures. *"If only I had listened…If only I had gone another way…If only I had paid more attention. If only…"*

Yeah…Then what? What would have happened? You don't know what the outcome would have been. It would probably be different from what you experienced but you still don't know. So why beat yourself up over it? What will that do besides make you feel bad? Why choose to feel lousy when you can choose to feel good?

We've all made mistakes or done things we wish we could have done differently. That's a part of growing up. A part of living life. A part of shaping who you are. It's not what happens that determines your future. It's what you do about what happens. Instead of dwelling on the negatives from the past, why not view them as a learning experience? At least now you know what to do differently or do better next time.

Thomas Edison went through many "failures" in his quest to create the light bulb. He failed at it at more than 1000 times. Yet he didn't consider his experiences as failures. Instead he viewed them as experiments. His positive outlook made a difference as he kept looking for ways to make his dream come true. Another example is the invention of the sticky note. One man's "failed" glue became the source of inspiration for another man's way to keep bookmarks in place without leaving a residue when removed. When the two scientists put their heads together, what initially seemed like a failed solution became what we know today as "post-it" notes.

As the saying goes, "With every adversity comes the seed of equal or greater opportunity." A lot of successful people today became successful because they chose to look at the silver lining in the dark cloud of each misfortune they encountered. Even in the direst circumstances, they were appreciative of what they had. Why? Because they know that regardless of how bad it was for them, it was worse for others. This positive outlook helped them to maintain their creative energy.

It's very hard to drive forward if you are focused on the rear view mirror instead of looking at what's in front of you. Unfortunately, we don't have the option to go back in time and change what happened. Life is not a trial run. It's the real deal. Therefore, if at first you don't succeed at something, dust yourself off and try again. It's not about how many times you fall. It's about how fast you bounce back.

The meaning we associate with the things we encounter has a great impact on how we let it affect us. How we internalize something has a lot to do with our thoughts, background, culture and our environment. In essence, it stems from our belief systems. If you're prone to having negative thoughts and being too hard on yourself, it's time to break that cycle. Recall past successes and be encouraged by them. Don't let your past rob you of your joy and self-confidence. If something didn't work out the way you wanted it to; just look at what you can learn from it. Take the lessons you can learn and move on. There are bigger and better things ahead. Just treat the past as a school, learn from your mistakes then press forward.

THE BEST IS YET TO COME

In contrast to people who beat themselves up over the past, many people relish in the "good old days" as if their future days are to be dreaded. They live in the memories of yesterday. To them, all the joys of life have already happened. Too often I hear people barely in their thirties and forties complaining and making comments like, "I'm too old to do that." Or they'll say, "If I knew what I know now, I would..."

It's good to re-live past memories and be encouraged by them. However, if that's all you do, where is your joy in living? Life is meant to be enjoyed and experienced each day. To make the most of every waking moment, you need to look at life as an adventure and plan fun activities that challenge you.

Have you ever noticed what happens to some people after they retire? Before long they get bored from not challenging their mind and staying active. After all, if all you live to do is play bingo all day long after living a life of exerting yourself, life may become less exciting.

On the other hand, there are some retired people who set goals. They pre-occupy themselves with meaningful projects and worthwhile activities beyond playing bingo. In doing so, they find happiness. They gain pleasure from spending time with their grandchildren, going for a walk, making clothes, volunteering or even reading.

To fully enjoy life, you need to have something good to look forward to. What is that one thing you would still like to do that you haven't done yet? Why not start taking baby steps towards it today?

Regardless of your age, live each day to the fullest. Instead of being stuck in the past, set goals so you can look forward to the future. It will make you more inspired to stick around and enjoy life!

NOTES

CHAPTER 6

GAIN STRENGTH FROM ADVERSITY

"Don't wish it was easier, wish you were better"
~ *Jim Rohn*

Everyone experience trials in one way or another. Yet, it's not merely the trials that make the difference; it's the people who face them. Two people could go through the exact same thing and yet respond differently. One may go as far as committing suicide, while the other calmly deals with the issue and slowly works his way out of the challenge. What makes the difference? The answer lies in each person's mental disposition.

If someone is optimistic and positive, he'll be better able to cope with stress. Though he may be going through a rough patch, he knows it's temporary. Just as the storms come and go; difficulties last for a while then they lessen or go away. There's always a silver lining behind the dark cloud. You just have to bear that in mind, even through the most challenging circumstance.

If someone is pessimistic or doesn't know how to handle stress well, he could end up taking drastic measures to end the test he's going through. He may go as far as taking his life. Even worse he may take the life of his family members, plus his own. When you hear of a man who kills his wife and kids then himself, the root cause is usually stress. In most cases, it's stress that stems from not having enough money. Though these are extreme examples, they happen all too often.

What steps can you take to ensure you can effectively handle stress? Let's look at some ways to gain strength from adversity and come out a winner.

TIPS TO HELP YOU COPE WITH PROLONGED STRESS OR HARDSHIP

1. Build your mental strength

A good way to build your mental strength and character is by developing the habit of reading ten pages of a good book per day. By a good book, I'm not talking about the tabloids or the latest online celebrity gossip. I'm referring to books that will encourage you to be a better person and help you develop strong character. Examples of good books include: *The Bible, The Seven Habits of Highly Effective People* and *How to Win Friends and Influence People*. Just about every major bookstore will have a copy of these books. If all else fails, you can order one or all of them from *Amazon.com* and have it delivered to your doorstep in the timeframe you desire.

Another good way to build your mental strength is

by listening to fifteen minutes of a good audio program or video program daily. You can listen to a CD or iPod while you drive and make good use of your time. The author of this book, Tony Robbins and Jim Rohn each has some great materials available. If you're short on cash, visit the library and lookup any of the books mentioned and start there. Try this suggestion for thirty days straight. You'll be amazed at the results!

2. Pray Regularly

When we look to God for help and guidance in dealing with trials, we invite him to bless us with inner peace. When we pray in faith, without doubting, we increase our ability to cope with stress.

I have personally experienced God's help in a stressful situation I had a work. I prayed incessantly for help to cope and I did my part to feed my mind with encouraging thoughts. I had full confidence that my prayer would be answered favorably. In time, my prayer was answered but it took faith and patience.

Sometimes we go through things that will test us. Sometimes our prayers may take a while to be answered. And sometimes the answers may come in a different way than we expect. In either case, prayer is a good way to relax your mind and give you the strength you need to get through the tough days.

3. Choose Your Friends Wisely

What does our choice of friends have to do with facing adversity? A lot more than you may think! Let's examine the effect that our friends can have on us. After all in times of stress, having someone to talk to and share our feelings with can mean the difference between seeing things through or giving up. I'm sure you've heard the phrase "birds of a feather flock together." This is true of us and our friends. People like people who are like themselves. It makes us comfortable. A friend can be regarded as a person who you know, like, and trust.

During difficult times, having good friends around you can strengthen you emotionally. Besides, doesn't it feel good to know other people love you and care about you? Since friends are so valuable, it makes sense to build good relationships with others, especially when things are going well for you. After all, who wants to be around someone who only comes around when they need something? Friendship is a two way street; it's a give and take. Both parties help each other.

Since friendship is so valuable does it mean everyone who comes along will be a good friend for you? The short answer is no, even if you may have some things in common. Sad to say, some people who befriend you may have selfish motives. Even if their motives are pure, their influence may not be for the better.

Hanging out with people who abuse substances like drugs or alcohol can negatively impact you, whether you believe it or not. That's why you have to choose your associates wisely. You may not allow someone to throw you off course but you may allow them to nudge you off course. Little by little they could get you to do things that go against your conscience and your values and before you know it, you could end up doing some questionable things.

Since friendship goes both ways, be there for your friends when they need you. Strive to be the best friend you can be. Just remember: *what goes around comes around. Whatever you sow, you will reap.* So plant good seeds by being a true friend. Then, when you need a friend, you'll reap what you sowed from being kind and considerate to your friends.

4. **Exercise Regularly**

How you feel about yourself will determine how well you cope with stress. Studies prove time and time again that regular exercise builds confidence and self-esteem. This in turn, affects how well you cope with a challenging situation. Though your physical muscles may hurt if you haven't exercised in a while, your mental muscles will leap for joy by how you feel afterwards.

A lot of people link exercise to weight loss. Losing weight is a good reason to exercise but is that all there is to it? Is vanity the only reason to stretch your muscles? Of course not! Exercising helps you to build muscle and improve your health both physically and emotionally. It can also help you out socially as you will most likely meet other people when you go for a walk or go to the gym. There are many other benefits to regular exercise, here are just a few:

1. Better Mood
2. Self Confidence
3. Stronger Muscles
4. Stronger Bones
5. Weight Control

6. Better Sleep
7. Increased Energy Level
8. Improved Immune System (prevents sickness)
9. More Flexible Body
10. Less Stress
11. Increased Brainpower and creativity

The key is to make the time to do some form of physical activity every day. It could be as simple as walking, biking or even doing house chores like mowing the lawn. Anything to get your heart rate up. Why not encourage a friend to join you? It doesn't matter how long you exercise just start building momentum. The more you do it, the easier it gets. Just get started!

5. Stay Positive & Look for Ways to Help Others

Above all else, you want to stay positive in your outlook as you undergo hardship. As mentioned earlier, keep looking for the silver lining in every dark cloud. This will help you to remain creative and focus your energy in the right direction and will make a difference for the better. As you apply the points shared in this chapter you will be able to look back on what you went through and smile knowing you successfully faced a challenging situation.

Make it a point to make other people feel good after being in your presence. When you're positive, people will gravitate towards you and will want to be in close contact with you. Why? Because you make them feel upbuilt. Instead of focusing on yourself and your problems, look for opportunities to compliment others sincerely. They will appreciate it and you will feel better too.

If you have the opportunity, volunteer your time for a worthy cause. This will take your mind off your challenges and help you to focus on helping others. By volunteering you can be a source of comfort to others and bring joy to their life when things look bleak.

CHAPTER 7

ENJOY LIFE EACH DAY

Let's escape for a moment. It's a pleasantly warm summer evening. The sky is pinkish orange as the sun sets beautifully across the sky. Like fluffy strands of cotton candy, the orange clouds stretch across the sky, daring you to touch it. As you stare in awe, a flock of black birds form a big "V" above your head as they search for a home for the night. You can hear them talking to each other in "bird language" as they each take turns to lead the pack. They do this to stay energized as they fly to their destination. As you take all this in, a state of relaxation and inner calm takes over and you're at peace inside. You're joyful for that moment of solitude, where you're able to collect your thoughts and reflect on the beauty around you.

Isn't it amazing how some of the simplest things can bring us great joy? Unfortunately, some people are so busy with the mundane things in life; they forget to find time to enjoy the simple things. Instead, they find a million reasons to postpone their joy. *I'm too busy. I have to do this and take care of that. I just can't find the time…* They're oblivious to the fact that where our focus goes, energy flows. They are so busy living a life without focus that they barely get through the day. Life is just this treadmill they're on; just going through the motions barely existing. But that doesn't have to be you…

If you're creative and is able to prioritize and put the more important things in their proper place, you can have a fulfilling life now. Not later when you "retire."

LOOK YOUR BEST!

It's important to look good because how you look affects how you feel. When you look your best, a smile comes naturally. So does your self-confidence. When you don't look your best, it's easy to become self conscious and insecure, wondering what other people think.

Make it a priority to feel good by wearing clean and dignified clothing that accentuates your skin tone and bring out your best features. It doesn't have to be the latest gadget, or the latest trend. It doesn't need to cost a fortune. It just needs to look good on you when you wear it. The joy and inner confidence that comes from looking and feeling good cannot be expressed in words. You don't have to be a shopaholic to look or feel good. You just have to learn how to feel comfortable in your own skin.

Do you receive a lot of compliments when you wear a certain color? Don't you tend to have more clothes in that color now? How about that nice pair of shoes you often get compliments on? Don't you tend to wear them more?

Since you never know who you may meet, make it a priority to look your best. When you look and feel your best, you'll likely to create a good impression on those you meet. More importantly do it for you!

Begin Each Encounter with a Smile

Have you ever made eye contact with a total stranger while you're walking? Isn't it sometimes awkward? You see each other coming down the way and you're both probably thinking, *"What am I going to do when I get near this person?"* As you walk closer and closer towards each other, you're faced with making that decision. Isn't it relieving when you actually say hi when you pass by?

Early one morning, I decided to go for a brisk walk before getting ready for work. It was about 5:15 in the morning. I was wide awake and was set on going for a walk since I had the energy. Off I went with a bottle of water in my hands enjoying the refreshing morning breeze. As I strolled along, all sorts of thoughts were going through my mind. Things I can't even recall now because as you know, we're always thinking about something.

I felt good as I went along, minding my own business, lost in my thoughts. As I continued my walk around the block, I came across a middle aged man. As I approached him, I thought about how I was going to greet him. I normally feel better when I greet someone as I pass them. However, if their head is held high and they purposely try to avoid making eye contact, I tend to just pass by without saying anything. It's one of those scenarios where you make a quick judgment call based on the situation. In any case, I had decided to take the initiative to say hi to this man as I passed him.

As I turned the corner along the sidewalk, this thin Indian man got closer in proximity to me. Before he was within three feet of me, I started to smile. As I got closer to him, he also smiled. He seemed very pleasant and somewhat religious. He was wearing a long, dress-like shirt and a pair of pants. Not the typical workout attire. His style of dress was typical of some religious Indian men. His long white beard and neatly wrapped turban also made me think he was of the Sikh faith. His pleasant smile and slight wave conveyed a true feeling of warmth and kindness. Naturally, I responded in kind. As we continued on our separate ways, that small gesture had a lasting, positive effect.

Perhaps you could make it a goal to begin each encounter with a smile. It has a way of putting you and others at ease. Why don't you try it today?

LIVE A LITTLE

Picture this. Your plane just landed in the Cayman Islands a few minutes ago and now you're finally at the hotel. The sun is shining. The sky is clear and the temperature is just right. As you look around, everyone seems relaxed as they smile contently. You're excited as you quickly head off for a nice massage.

You've waited a long time to pamper yourself like this and being at one of the most sought after hotels makes it even more exciting. Anticipation floods your heart as you head towards the spa. In no time you're laying flat on your belly, relaxed as can be. All your cares and worries start to fade away. Before you know it, you're in wonderland savoring the pleasant aroma of the candles and welcoming the gentle touch of the masseuse. With each stroke, your tense muscles start to loosen as your pores soak in the sweet smelling massage oil. In the background you can hear the relaxing music. Gradually, you enter a state of bliss and utter relaxation. Your mind is clear of everything. As you're being pampered, you think to yourself, "This is just wonderful!"

The good news is there are countless ways to "live a little" without having to go to an exotic country in the Caribbean. *You can pamper yourself right at home.* You don't need to be rich; you just need to be creative.

Instead of postponing your happiness, make it a point to enjoy life now. Here a few ideas on how to do just that…

1. Be spontaneous (go for a hike or get out of town for a quick weekend trip).
2. Go to the beach or by the lake – a nice view of the water can work wonders.
3. Buy that dress or shoes that you've had your eyes on.
4. Have a bite of your favorite chocolate.
5. Go to the opera, the movies, or that nice restaurant
6. Take yourself on a long drive or go with a buddy on a road trip, as you listen to your favorite music.
7. Escape in that book you've been meaning to read.

8. Go on that cruise your friends have been raving about.
9. Have some friends over for a nice meal.

There are countless other ways to live a little. These are just a few suggestions to get you started. Feel free to act on any other ideas you can think of.

TAKE CHARGE OF YOUR OWN HAPPINESS!

Real joy and happiness comes from engaging in activities that make you feel good. Have you ever noticed that when you are laughing or smiling genuinely, it's hard to be upset?

A lot of people play the "blame game" and find everyone else at fault if their life is miserable. More often than not you hear, *I can't do that because he won't let me…or…She won't let me do that!*

Make it a point to take responsibility for how you live your life. Blaming others will weaken you. Whereas taking responsibility will empower you. Your happiness is too important to be left to chance or be dependent on someone else. Have fun, enjoy life and stay clear of negative people!

NOTES

CHAPTER 8

Keep Growing & Improving

"The only way of finding the limits of the possible is by going beyond them into the impossible."
~ Arthur C. Clarke

How does a person become a great pianist? Isn't it by studying the keyboard and playing the notes repeatedly? To get really good at it comes at a price, not just in terms of money. Besides acquiring the piano and tuning it, there is a price to pay to learn how to play and master the instrument.

To get really good at anything, you have to give up something. It could be scaling back on one of your hobbies. It could be limiting shopping or cutting back on how long you talk or text on the phone. To master the fundamentals of your trade or craft, you will need to take the right steps to get really good. Here are some practical steps to help you in your quest to develop your talents:

1. Cultivate the desire to get better
2. Honor your promises
3. Build and protect your good name
4. Do what you love and strive to be your best
5. Cultivate the right attitude
6. Lead by example

1. **Cultivate the Desire to Get Better**

Since we don't live in a perfect world, perfection will always be something we strive for. Regardless of how good you get, you can't get complacent. The minute you do, is the minute you stop growing. In life, nothing stays the same. You're either growing or regressing. That's why you have to position your actions so that time is working for you instead of against you.

Since preparing, rehearsing or practicing isn't always fun, you have to develop the desire to "want to" do it. When the desire is there, it will be a lot easier to prepare in advance. You have to develop a strong resolve for what you want so that it will fuel you even on the days when you 'want to' but don't have the energy. When you develop the habit of acting in harmony with your goals, the momentum that you build in the beginning will become sustainable later on. Before you know it, you'll be on "auto-pilot", and will end up just doing what you need to do without even thinking about it.

I was recently listening to the story of a woman who went to play golf with about thirty men. She was the only woman on the golf course. The players were divided into teams and she ended up on a team with four other men. All the teams were comprised of men only, except for hers. A few of the men on her team started squirming when they saw she was on their team. Right away they thought the woman would make them lose. As much as we may try to deny it, some guys still view women as "soft" and incapable, especially when they're surrounded by other guys. Much to their surprise, she did better than them on the golf course. Plus, their team did better than the other teams because she was on the team. She pushed them to newer heights and earned their respect by the end of the game.

What made her successful? She practiced a lot prior to that game! She lived the motto: practice, practice, practice. By practicing she gained the confidence she needed and was able to live up to her own expectations of herself. She saw herself as a winner before she got on the course. She did what she needed to do to prepare in advance so the ball would do what she wanted, when she wanted it to. She visualized the winning moment long in advance and that enabled her to feel comfortable in her own skin, even when her team mates were making her feel unwelcomed. Due to her advanced preparation, she was then able to draw on her reservoir of inner strength in the midst of feeling awkward and uncomfortable. Repetition is the mother of skills. This is something she was well of aware of. As a result, she honed her skills prior to playing the game by practicing when no one else was watching. What she did in private, paid off in public.

Say you want a more toned physique than the one you have now. A key to reach that goal would be regular exercise. The more you do it, the easier and more enjoyable it will become. As exercising becomes a source of pleasure to you,

you'll end up doing it without even thinking about it. In no time you'll develop the lean muscles that you want. Staying toned and looking good is the natural result that happens as a by-product from exercising regularly.

Regardless of your goal, you can be successful if you prepare ahead and do what it takes to get the results you seek. You have to be willing to do what you can to be better prepared than anyone else. How? Just learn to view practice as an opportunity, instead of an obligation. It's an opportunity to be the best you can be and master your skills. As you get better, you'll enjoy it more. At first it may not be as much fun but if you keep reminding yourself of why you're doing it, staying the course will become much easier. Plus your advanced preparation will give you the confidence you need to do well, come game time. Regardless of what you're doing, give it your all. Go the extra mile, even in the practice sessions. Master the fundamentals.

To keep things interesting, you can break up your practice routines into chunks. Identify specific things that you want to get good at. This will enable you to practice with a purpose. Set goals for yourself even in your practice sessions. As you compare your results, you'll boost your confidence by the small wins that come from hitting your goals. You might even get a log book or journal to track your progress as you go along.

2. **Honor Your Promises**

For every promise, there's a price. It requires commitment to stick to a promise whether to yourself or someone else. As Jeff Olson puts it, "Commitment is doing the thing that you said you would do, long after the feeling that you said it in has left you." It's very easy to do things when you're in a peak state and ready to go. But what happens when you cool off? After all, some days we may just not be in the mood, even though you know what you need to do.

Have you ever made a promise that you sincerely meant to follow through on but didn't? Perhaps your circumstances changed or you didn't foresee the full price you'd have to pay for your promise. Because stuff happens, sometimes it may be difficult to follow through on your word. However, we strengthen our character when we deliver on our word; even when it's not convenient.

When it comes to promises you make to yourself, turn your 'shoulds' into 'musts'. If you need to make a call, make it a must. If it's just a 'should', you'll blow it off as something to get around to. If you 'must' make that call, you'll just do it. Everybody gets what they must have. It becomes a survival thing. That's how strong your resolve becomes when you make it a must. It becomes non-negotiable. A lot of people never follow through on personal goals because they view them merely as something they "should" do. *I should go to the gym. I should lose weight. I should save more money. I should, I should, I should…* As Tony Robbins would put it, "They should all over themselves." You don't want to do that, do you? Then turn your shoulds into musts and get them done.

3. **Build and Protect Your Good Name**
   "A name is to be chosen rather than abundant riches; favor is better than even silver and gold."
   ~ *King Solomon*

Credit. A simple word with a lot of meaning behind it. This could refer to having a good reputation that carries "weight". Having a good name helps in all aspects of life. People will likely give you the time of day if they hear good things about you. Just like anything else that's worthwhile, building a good name comes at a price. On the days when you don't feel like honoring a commitment but you do it anyway, you make a deposit towards building up a good reputation.

In the financial world, credit is defined as "confidence in a purchaser's ability and intention to pay, displayed by entrusting the buyer with goods or services without immediate payment." You've probably heard the terms 'good credit' or 'bad credit' used pretty often. The type of credit you have boils down to the reputation you establish. If you establish a good track record of honoring your word and paying back what you borrow, you will earn the trust and respect of people who don't know you and you will establish good credit. On the other hand, if you break your promises and prove unreliable in repaying what you borrow, you'll build a bad name credit-wise and will have bad credit.

But what if your good name got dinged or suffered a major blow? Don't give up! It's never too late to do the right thing and re-establish your name. It will just take time. How fast you get back on your feet and restore your good name will depend on a few factors like what created the damage and the severity of the damage. In either case, time will be your best ally. Say for example you went through some challenges and your credit is less than perfect. To strengthen your borrowing power you may choose to set a goal to re-establish and re-build your credit. Will that happen overnight? Certainly not!

Just as it took a while for your credit to become damaged, it will take some time to repair. However, each time you pay back your creditors in a timely way, you re-establish your good name and open the door to other opportunities in the future.

Though we live in a world where instant gratification is the order of the day, the principle of the seasons still hold true. First you plant...then cultivate...then harvest. A lot of people want to skip the middle step, the cultivating part. It's a pity they don't know that this is a key component before you can get the results of the harvest. As you cultivate your "farm" to restore your name, focus on the reward. This will keep you going when you feel like giving up. It will give you energy when you're ready to give up. Plus it will add fuel when your drive starts to dwindle. Just remember: for every promise, there's a price. Time is a part of the price.

4. Do What You Love & Strive to Be Your Best

To keep growing, you must strive to get as close to perfection as you can in each undertaking. You may not reach perfection but the key is in the striving. If you set your goals high and you miss, you will still do well. However, if you strive to be average, you'll fall below average if you miss. That's why it's better to aim high. We tend to live up to our own expectations so strive to be the best.

Take a good look at your strengths and your weaknesses. Spend most of your time building on your strengths. Practice being the best you can be. Take your own capabilities into consideration and strive for something above that. This will keep you humble and keep you from being bored. The only way to learn the extent of what you can do is by doing your best and constantly challenging yourself. As you do this, you'll develop your confidence and self-image.

5.   Cultivate the right Attitude

Attitude is everything. What you expect is what you get. If you expect to do well, you will. If you expect to fail, you will. Play with your all. Leave nothing on the table. Give it your best, no matter what you are attempting. A positive can-do attitude is critical for success. It's not developed overnight. It takes time. Make a habit of saying nice things to yourself throughout the day. Nice things like:

> *Today is a great day, I'm excited to get started on my goals.*
> *I am happy and grateful now that I've seen the sunrise.*
> *I can tackle whatever challenges are ahead of me.*

It might be uncomfortable at first but just do it. Do it often. Do it daily. It will put you in the right frame of mind.

6.   Lead by Example

Becoming a true leader requires that you work on leading yourself before you can lead others. Develop the leader in you by walking your talk. Model others who have walked the path you're looking to trod. Learn what you can from them. No one person will have all the answers, so keep an open mind and look for admirable qualities in several mentors. We all have different gifts. As leaders we need to acknowledge the gifts in others and work with them to bring out the best in each other.

To inspire others, you need to lead by example. You will first have to perform at the level you want others to perform at. You will also need to treat others the way you would like to be treated. As a leader, you have to muster up the courage to take the risk and go where you haven't been before.

Create an environment of trust, especially with those you encounter on a daily basis: at home, at work or at school. Do things that you believe in. If you believe what you're doing is right, it will be easier to convey that belief with sincerity.

Listen to others. By listening attentively you show respect to the person who is speaking. By showing respect, you will be able to earn their respect. It's one of those things that goes both ways. When others respect you, they'll be more willing to give you the time of day when you want them to hear you out. So lead by example by being a good listener.

Learn to handle pressure by handling one thing at a time. This will help you to develop into a strong leader...someone worth following. A mentor of mine once said, "If you want to know if you're a real leader, look who is following you. If no one is behind you, you're just going for a walk." How well you handle difficulties will show your strength of character and will encourage others to put faith in you. As you learn to manage pressure, focus on taking each challenge in stride. Multiple small wins lead to big wins down the line.

Competition is a good thing sometimes. The better your opponents are, the better you have to be. Use this pressure as a source of energy. This will help you to successfully navigate through change when you're confronted with it. When things are challenging and stressful, keep your cool. The more you prepare, the easier it will be to handle the unplanned and unexpected when they creep up. Though you can't prepare for everything, if you learn to take things for what they are and not exaggerate them, it will be easier to manage stress and encourage others to believe in you.

Smile often. When you smile, you show your endearing side. Your pleasant smile and warm personality will help you to attract the success you want and will draw others to you.

NOTES

CLOSING THOUGHTS

Throughout this book you learned some ways to take charge of your life and go for your dreams. Now it's up to you to act on what you learned. Nothing will change unless you change. To get different results you have to do things differently. The ideas shared in this book will bear results when you apply them. Read it again to refresh your memory and reinforce the eight steps presented. Just remember, you have the ability to dictate how your life is written. It's your time for a new beginning.